THE WORLD RESTORED

Jonathan Lever www.archilever.com

RE-POPULATING THE WORLD WITH ANIMALS
TO BRING BACK A GARDEN OF EDEN

The world Restored…re-populating the world with Animals to bring back a garden of Eden…….

The world is ever changing, and one thing is for sure, is the continuous stream of people into larger cities. The ongoing surge for larger and larger urbanisation at least in my view is disconnecting the younger generations from this world in many ways. Hundreds of millions of children, adolescents and adults now are brought up in concrete jungles in effect – disconnected from Nature. The smells of car fumes, storm water drains, sewer smells rising from drains, the 24hr noise and buzz of traffic, dodgy cars and buses on busy roads are their daily experiences. Visually surrounded by concrete, glass and metal buildings, roads, sirens, pavements, crime, grime, hard edges, the general lack of views in large cities, and plugged into a lifetime cycle of money makes the world go round. Even though I'm an Architect by training and career mostly, I generally find most large cities horrible, I really don't like big cities for more than short visits. They of course can look spectacular at night when you cant see most of it, and the lights give a sense of magic to the city. I know too that cities offer many cool activities and things to do – great galleries, museums, theatres etc etc and I think that cities certainly have their uses to a point and are good from those points of view, but the ever growing urbanisation and mega cities, as I've written about in some of my other books are in fact turning their back on humanity in many ways, and we are seeing more and more large cities in fact creating poverty – vertical slums, smaller and smaller apartments, people cramming in to places – some horror scenes really.

I think in many ways humans have lost their way with this lust for urbanisation and big cities. We are loosing valuable connections with nature – and I think that it is vital for children to be offered that connection – we owe it to them in fact.

Nature provides us with so much and the connection to it cannot be underestimated – especially for children. It is no coincidence that we are placed on this earth surrounded by nature – its almost that people have been choosing to turn away from that and go towards more concrete and lifeless cities – as I already said, I'm not knocking the excitement of cities, sure its definitely there, but the hellish nature of overcrowded cities with traffic is simply anti logic – like where are we going with this? I've been to Hong Kong and to various multi storey high rise complexes in China and other cities, and to me at least, its pretty close to hell as we can get really.

And you feel different in nature. Even human behaviour shows us this – peoples responses are everywhere – people watch sunsets, people go to the beach, people go to the mountains, people go to nature as holidays to get away from cities. In fact they pay vast sums of money to do this in many cases – so why are humans loosing that contact with nature. And if nature now has such a premium attached to it – normally financially too – then we have missed something. And nature is not just about trees, landscapes, sunsets, mountains etc etc – a huge part of the nature experience are animals and birds. Even in built up cities the amount of pet keeping is significant. People find a calming effect by being with animals – be it whatever pet – dogs, cats, birds, reptiles etc etc

Animals open our senses in a different way than just watching television. Animals create a presence and also in most cases bring out emotions and heighten our senses. Animals can pick up peoples moods, make them feel calm, make them feel love, make them feel peace, happiness. So the power of animals is well known in many cultures, right across the world.

The combination though of nature in the form of trees, landscapes, bush, plus animals then makes for such a powerful influence on humans.

The uplifting feeling people get from visiting games parks in Africa, being in real natural bush surroundings, smelling the plants, the trees, the smell of the air is unique, it has a kind of herbal smell, then the tranquillity that comes from being in those natural surroundings is priceless – well of course its nature – you add wildlife to those natural surroundings, then you get all sorts of new dimensions to how it impacts humans.

Its difficult to fully describe these things and of course it affects people differently. But suffice to say, if you're bumping into people on a busy pavement, trying to cross heavy traffic, its hardly the same as being in nature watching sunsets and animals roaming free.

The connection people have always had with nature has been for the vast majority of populations, slowly, bit by, severed, diminished to in many cases not at all and in most cases become a luxury to get away to.

I know that now cities are all formed, and become such big monsters that it is going to be difficult to rewind these factors, and in many cases next to impossible -the over urbanisation has already happened. But there are vast areas away from cities and on the edges, which are still green areas, green spaces. There is definitely room for looking beyond a pocket type approach, a chance to look at a more worldly view on some matters regarding nature – and this is what this book is mostly about. I want to use this book as a taster, discussion point, thought provoker, a short set of suggestions to bring about a worldwide radical intervention to radically increase and mass breed wild animals and birds to re-populate ethe earth with animals and birds as it would have been before humans came in and pretty much hunted things out. There have been unbelievable amounts of hunting and killing of animals over the centuries, and I am suggesting it would be wonderful to re-populate the levels of animals right across the world on a gigantic scale.

Amongst many things this book will suggest how that could happen. I will give ideas and concepts to that. In a word picture though what I'm suggesting would be a long the lines of large breeding and distribution centres across the world, where animals would be carefully bred in large numbers with the view of repopulating the world with staggering numbers of animals so in effect all the wild areas and even up to parks and green areas will have animals in them, so children and people are back in direct contact with nature. Even in Africa where there are animals roaming free in their natural habitat, centuries of hunting by humans has seriously diminished animal numbers. They used to be everywhere is large numbers – literally right across Africa it was teaming with wildlife – that has changed – and I want this to be reverted back to how things were – where the whole world has wildlife everywhere – sort of like the beginning times. The world will then be a fantastic place, like a fantasy continuous wildlife park, with animals and birds everywhere, instead of scattered in little pockets.

This book is going to suggest we address this imbalance and restore the glory of what the earth was like in effect.

The ideas I will propose are quite easy to do, and will be practical suggestions. I am hoping too that this will in time also then get rid of zoos – which are actually pretty cruel in my view – the Sydney zoo has large African animals that should be roaming free in large areas, not couped up in pens. So the ideas and suggestions in this book could radically change the world for the better – certainly for future generations. I think people will generally be better off living in the world as it was intended to be anyway. Not all crammed into big filthy concrete jungles which are in any case I believe now driving poverty in every major city. I have written about this extensively in my other book – I will highlight that in this book too.

The Darker side of Humans and Animals:

Throughout history, people have killed animals. For a number of reasons – sometimes out of protection, self defence, safety and well being of their livestock. The obvious next factor being food – survival, and of course for their skins. I'm not going to argue for or against this, as every situation is different I guess and history has put people in all sorts of situations, and survival is one of those. Survival makes humans do all sorts of things.
But I have looked back at numerous historical pictures from archives and one finds in the past early settlers in areas went on some mind blistering hunts – wholesale slaughter. I've seen piles of ivory, animals skins – such large numbers you simply cannot believe what you're seeing. Certainly in Zimbabwe and South Africa in the early days of settlement by westerners, staggering amounts of wildlife was pretty much wholesale slaughtered. The pictures I have seen are simply shocking.

But lets fast forward to modern times and this has turned into a very devilish enterprise – in places like south Africa and Zimbabwe, greedy foreign currency hungry companies and individuals have been shooting animals with stupid tourists for years. Its big quick fast money – people are paying thousands and thousands of dollars to pull a trigger at an elephant or kudu or lion. Its pure greed. Nothing less than that. Its basically criminal in my view. The world was populated with animals in vast numbers before man embarked on decimating wildlife pretty much across the planet, so any stories or bs propaganda that hunting helps maintain numbers or help the planet in any way are just blatant lies. All trophy hunting is driven by monumental human greed, and run by serious scum bags in my view. It makes me sick to the stomach hearing all these numb nuts boasting about shooting leopards, elephants etc etc. I just don't get it. People getting kicks and thrills out of killing beautiful wildlife. It madness.

Old days mass killing / slaughter of animals

I guess long back in history when there was so much wildlife around people could foresee the damage it was going to do to the future animals populations across the world

Old days mass killing / slaughter of animals

Old days mass killing / slaughter of animals

Old days mass killing / slaughter of animals

Modern poaching / slaughter

In modern times this extremely shameful routine continues – we see international hunters coming from afar to places like Africa to shoot animals for kicks. Mostly trophy's. We are fed this big bs lie that oh it helps conservation and that the funds are used for conservation – a bigger lie would be hard to find – all it is unscrupulous hunting companies cashing in on large sums of foreign currency, fast and furious for doing nothing more than kill animals for fun. Its pure greed.

Modern poaching / slaughter

Killing for kicks and thrills

Modern poaching / slaughter

Killing for kicks and thrills

Modern poaching / slaughter

Killing for kicks and thrills

Modern poaching / slaughter

Killing for kicks and thrills

Modern poaching / slaughter

Killing for kicks and thrills

Modern poaching / slaughter

Killing for kicks and thrills

Modern poaching / slaughter

Killing for kicks and thrills

Modern poaching / slaughter

I'm not sure what goes on in the minds of people like this – perhaps they feel macho or something. It really would have been better if the Trump boys had never set foot in Africa to be quite blunt – what a disgrace – they're not welcome back – ever.

Killing for kicks and thrills

Killing for kicks and thrills

Senseless killing – all for stupid thrills – no morals really – if you needed to eat - ok

Killing for kicks and thrills

Killing for kicks and thrills

These people are all sick in the mind really

Killing for kicks and thrills

Time to re-plan and re-stock the world's Wildlife – any new cities look at greenbelts which run through cities like rivers in effect

Architects, urban designers, planners, businessmen etc are always looking at big new trends, such as smart cities, pedestrian cities, futuristic cities etc etc – and while they're always smart ideas and well thought out, it could be a great ideas for future generations to start looking at any new cities having massive greenbelts through them, and in fact planning cities around them to bring back proper numbers of wildlife. Instead of paying large sums of money to go across the world to game parks, we should be living in and around nature. We need to think about flipping all the narratives on how urban planning and cities are thought through. Let me show you some examples of how awful cities are becoming to live in in areas – this is not how humans are supposed to live – this is verging on economic slavery in my view – and the poor children that have to be brought up in this diabolical system – its hell really – this is not how the world was intended for us to live in – so why are we allowing idiots in planning, governments to let this mess carry on – it has to change really if wee are going to be responsible people and give the future generations of children a good start in life. Cities are not good for bringing up children – full stop – no debate – they're fine for visiting – but day to day living – massively built up cities are simply hell holes for children. Living in smelly concrete jungles, with no to little greenery is simply a disaster for children and adults to be quite blunt again. Cities have their limits. Humans with limited exposure to nature is not a good thing at all. I will start by showing you a few examples of these hell hole scenarios – there are many more.

Hell on earth – simply that – this is slavery

**Humans were never ever meant to be living like this –
these kind of developments are crimes against
humanity really – I cant explain them otherwise**

Nature? What nature? - a nightmare for children

Planning cities with proper greenbelts and wildlife for the future..

Cities should have proper greenbelts that run through with plants, trees, water and teaming with wildlife

Planning cities with proper greenbelts and wildlife for the future..

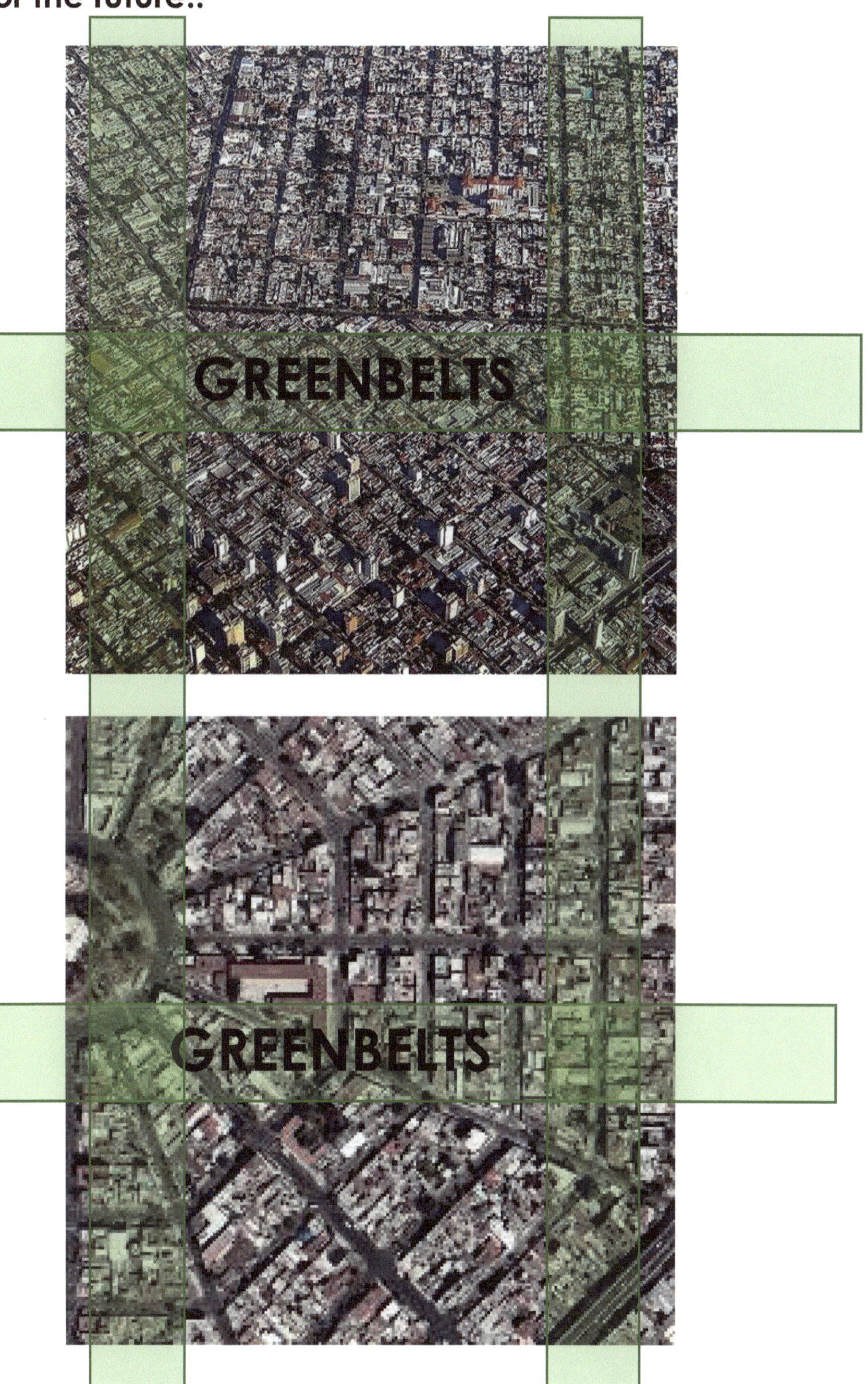

Proper flowing integrated green areas filled with wildlife relevant to each world regions climate and natural stocks

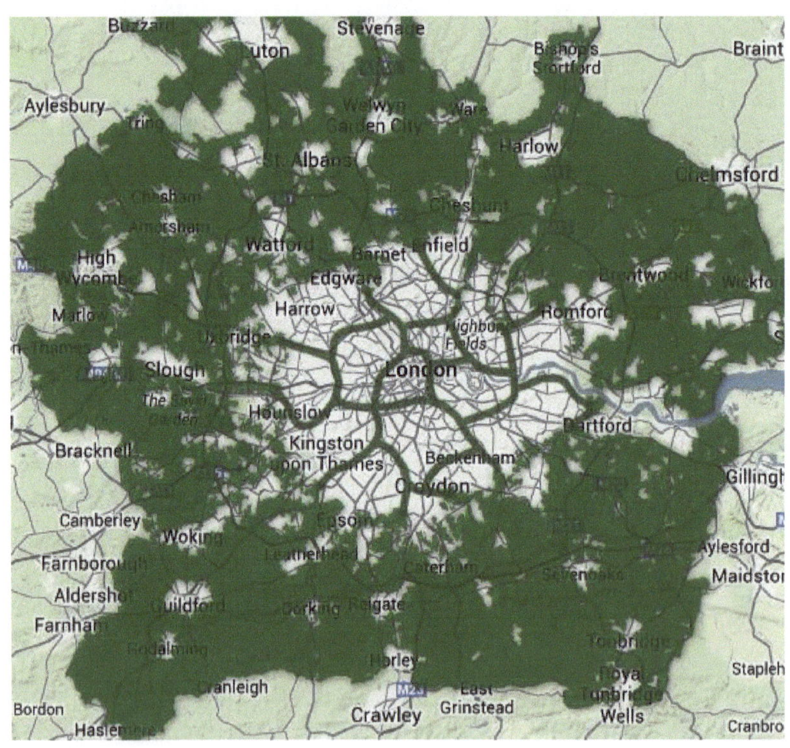

In every country – multiple wildlife breeding centres will be needed of every size – using the existing ones and new mega centres – almost like big game farms. Breeding at full pace

A worldwide, concerted effort, with huge funding to establish not only continuous wildlife greenbelts, but also gigantic breeding centres right across the world

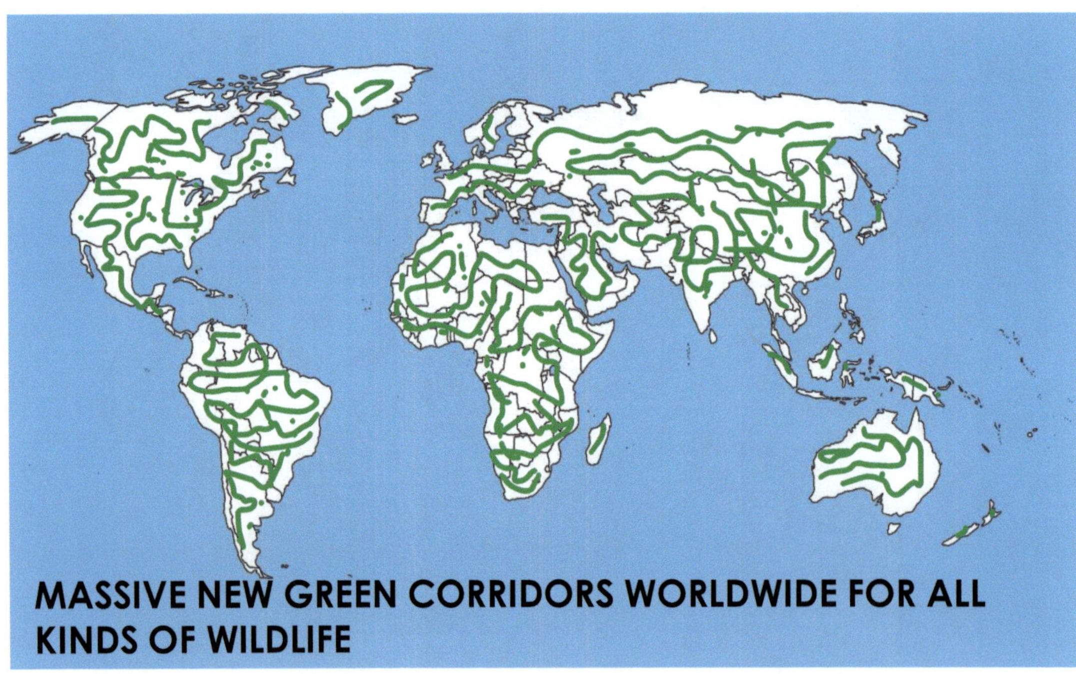

The scale of this worldwide project would need the complete shutdown of current idiotic politicians spending trillions on destructive wars and genocide and for large portions of those funds to be re-directed into this kind of project – the pentagon for example has spent in the last three decades over 40 trillions dollars on basically a worldwide exercise on killing people, destroying countries and cities, where as those funds could be far better spent on building a worldwide greenbelt system teaming with wildlife – whereby children and families could reconnect with nature as intended – we as humans I believe should all be living in a garden of Eden type setting naturally – not paying large sums of money to travel to them as a luxury. When we came to earth – the earth and all its resources were free – where did we go wrong as humans.

Lets make this world a better place. Lets restore nature the way its meant to be. Lets replan new developments accordingly